Lee's Tapestry Works

Life and Work in the North End of Birkenhead

Alan Johnson and Kevin Moore

First published 1987 by the Departments of Economic History and Sociology, University of Liverpool

This Edition published 2002 by Liver Press
14 Appin Road, Birkenhead, Merseyside, CH41 9HH

British Library Cataloguing in Publication Data.
A Catalogue record for this book is available from the British Library.

ISBN 1 871201 11 X

Printed and Typeset by Birkenhead Press Limited,
14 Appin Road, Birkenhead, Merseyside, CH41 9HH

Contents

Source of Illustrations
All the illustrations used are by courtesy of the Williamson Art Gallery, Birkenhead, except for the following: Elsie Joinson (page 38), Mrs. E. Hotchkiss (page 52), Jessie Halewood (page 60), Gladys Rimmer (pages 73 and 78), Stephen Lee (page 74), Tony Lee (page 74).

This book is sponsored by

Friends of the Williamson Art Gallery
& Wirral Museums

Friends of the Williamson Art Gallery & Wirral Museums

The Friends was set up as a registered charity over 20 years ago to support the work of the museums run by Wirral Borough Council, the list of which has expanded considerably since the organisation began. It now embraces: Williamson Art Gallery & Museum; Birkenhead Priory & St Mary's Tower; Wirral Museum at Birkenhead Town Hall, incorporating Wirral Archives Service; Shore Road Pumping Station; Egerton Bridge; Taylor Street Bus & Tram Heritage Centre, and Birkenhead Tramways.

The Friends contributes to the costs of hospitality at exhibition private views, to which Friends are invited, organises a very popular season of concerts and contributes towards children's and other activities within the museums, and supports purchases for the museums collections and to aid the work of museums staff.

Subscription rates are modest and members receive an occasional newsletter, invitations and information on events, and a warm glow of satisfaction that their involvement can make a difference.

Details from the Friends of WAG & WM
c/o Williamson Art Gallery & Museum
Slatey Road
Birkenhead
CH43 4UE

Telephone: 0151 652 4177

Friends of the Williamson Art Gallery & Wirral Museums is a Registered Charity no. 514641.

Acknowledgements to Original Edition

This book simply could not have been put together without the help of literally hundreds of people who used to work at Lee's. To list all of those who have loaned photographs, given their memories, or offered material for the exhibition would be impossible. Thanks to you all.

David Hillhouse, Colin Simpson and the staff of the Williamson Art Gallery have helped a great deal from the start. They have kindly allowed us the use of their large collection of Lee's photographs and archives, and have also given much sound advice. Thanks also to National Museums and Art Galleries on Merseyside. Thanks also to local author, Bill Houldin, for pointing us in the right direction. Many thanks also to the workers at the Birkenhead Unemployed Centre for their help. We are very grateful to Ian Qualtrough and Susan Yee of the Photographic Unit at Liverpool University for all the work they have done for us. Thanks also to Patricia McMillan and Diane Murgatroyd for typing the manuscript at such short notice, and to Val Taylor for design and typesetting. Finally, we want to thank Pat Ayers, our co-worker, and Bob Lee and Tony Lane, the project directors, for their help and encouragement.

Alan Johnson
Kevin Moore

Preface to 2002 Edition

Lee's Tapestry Works was originally published by the Departments of Economic History and Sociology, the University of Liverpool, under the title 'The Tapestry Makers'.

This title was the first of several resulting from research carried out as part of a project called the Merseyside Docklands Community History Project whose brief was to collect and preserve photographs, mementos and memories of life and industry so that a record of the dockland communities would be preserved for future generations.

The original team, Pat Ayres, Alan Johnson and Kevin Moore have all moved on to pastures new and the booklets they originally produced have been out of print for some years.

The School of History at Liverpool University still publishes local material in association with Liverpool John Moores University and Countyvise Limited as 'Liver Press'.

It seemed appropriate for Liver Press to re-publish the Docklands History titles and 'Athol Street' was re-printed in 1998. Now 'The Tapestry Makers' is being reprinted with a slightly changed title to reflect more specifically its subject.

While the Acknowledgements have been reproduced as they appeared in the original edition, the publishers of this edition wish to acknowledge the help and sponsorship of the *Friends of the Williamson Art Gallery and Wirral Museums*. Helen Kermode of *Groundwork, Wirral* has provided the Epilogue which brings the story right up to date. We thank her for her contribution.

LEE~FABRICS

Prologue

On October 25th 1986 over 450 people gathered at the Williamson Art Gallery, Birkenhead. Nearly all had one thing in common. They had worked at Lee's Tapestry Works in Stanley Road, Birkenhead. This was the first 'reunion' since the factory closed in 1970.

The event was organised by the Docklands History Project, with the help of the Williamson Art Gallery. Three months previously a study had begun of the history of the Tapestry Works, with a view to producing an exhibition. We appealed, in the local press, for ex-Lee's workers to help us. Their response was tremendous. Over one hundred got in touch with offers of photographs, fabrics and most importantly, memories. Wishing to, but being unable to see everyone, it was decided to organise the reunion.

The afternoon was spent looking at old photographs of the works, and watching old films of the factory and its holiday camp in North Wales. The ex-workers could also see samples of many of the fabrics they had made and some of the tools they had used to make them. Above all it was an opportunity to renew old friendships and a chance to remember. It was an emotional day.

Chapter 1. From Bolton to Birkenhead

Lee's Tapestry Works, or the 'Tap' as it was known by its workers, was a unique place. From 1908 until its closure in 1970, this factory in Stanley Road, Birkenhead, produced luxurious tapestries and embroideries for some of the finest buildings around the world. Lee's fabrics can still be found in stately homes, palaces, embassies, boardrooms and luxury hotels in many different countries. They have been used to furnish the White House in Washington and the Royal Train in which King George VI toured southern Africa in 1947. In 1936, the firm received a 4000 yard order for fabrics to decorate the ocean liner the 'Queen Mary', and many other Cunard liners were furnished with Lee's fabrics. Some of Lee's products were prodigious works of art. An order for the boardroom of the Midland Bank in London required 15.5 million stitches, and took 7.5 months to complete. The labour involved was the equivalent of 4 months work by 54 women. One single panel of this order measured 70 feet 8 inches by 12 feet 8 inches, and is believed to be the largest needlework tapestry ever produced.

Yet in its heyday, most people outside Birkenhead itself were unaware of Lee's existence. Other Merseysiders know little or nothing about the firm, or what it was like to work there. Most people have probably seen a Lee's fabric in a stately home, without recognising it as such. No doubt one of the reasons why Lee's remained largely unknown even before its closure was because its products were far beyond the means of most people. Certainly no Lee's employees could afford to furnish their homes with the fabrics some of them had spent perhaps forty years of their lives making!

Perhaps the firm also remains largely forgotten because most of those who worked there were women; there were about seven women for every one man. Like so many aspects of the lives of women in the past, women's work in factories, particularly before the Second World War, has either been ignored or seen as less significant than the work of men. The work of women and men at Lee's should be remembered, not least because it involved a high degree of craft skill. In many departments workers were not considered to be fully trained until they had been with the firm for five years, though none of them served what was officially termed an apprenticeship.

Tapestries made in Birkenhead? It seems an unlikely combination, and one would have expected a firm making such fabrics to have been based in either the Lancashire or Yorkshire textile centres. In fact, Arthur Lee, the founder of the Tapestry Works, originally came from Bolton, and the story of how he came to Birkenhead is a complicated one.

Arthur Henry Lee was born in 1853. His family was already well-known in the textile industry, his father Henry being one of the first partners of the famous firm Tootal Broadhurst Lee. At the age of eighteen Arthur was put in charge of a spinning mill owned by the firm. Later he managed one of the large Bolton cotton mills owned by the company, and this mill had over 500 looms producing plain calico cloth. However, Arthur Lee was already more interested in weaving tapestry, and for this purpose he had four or five jacquard looms at the mill. This interest was probably stimulated by his brother-in-law, G.F. Armitage, an architect and designer, who supplied most of the early designs. Armitage was connected with William Morris, the socialist and designer, and it is clear that Arthur Lee was influenced by Morris' artistic views if not his political ones. For Morris, the Victorian era was a 'philistine age' of conformity and shoddiness in the products which · filled even the homes of the rich: "It is a shoddy age. Shoddy is king. From the statesman to the shoemaker, all is shoddy." In the 1860s he had set up a firm to produce a wide range of products, from furniture and wallpaper to tapestries and embroideries, using traditional and often long forgotten craft skills. Walter Crane, the Liverpool-born artist, summed up this new movement in the following words:

"in design; a return to simplicity, to sincerity, to good materials and sound workmanship; to rich and suggestive surface decoration and simple constructive forms."

It was on these lines that Arthur Lee set out to make tapestries.

Arthur Henry Lee, the founder of the Tapestry Works (1853-1932).

Lee's works at Warrington, about 1900.

1887 was a year of depression in the cotton industry, and the Bolton mill was losing money. This was the stimulus for Arthur Lee to set up his own firm to produce woven tapestries only. The jacquard looms were moved to Warrington in 1888, to a corner of one of the cotton mills owned by his wife Caroline's family. By 1890 the firm had opened a sales office in London, but Arthur Lee believed that the United States would be the prime market for his products. In 1903 his eldest son, Thorold, established a sales office in New York, which was taken over two years later by Arthur's second son, Humphrey, who settled in America. In 1904, Christopher, the youngest son, entered the business. About this time the family moved to West Kirby, due to the poor health of Caroline Lee. For a time Arthur and his sons commuted each day to Warrington, but in 1908 a new factory was opened in the north end of Birkenhead. The jacquard looms were brought from Warrington by horse and cart. Several of the women weavers also moved with the firm, such as Annie McCann, Alice Clayton and Clara Knight, and two mechanics, Isaac Wilkinson and Jack Armitage.

Aerial view of the Works, 1936. Note the Dock Cottages at the bottom of the photograph.

It may seem an unlikely reason for a factory to move, but the new location did have a lot to recommend it. There were good transport links, being close to Dock Station (Birkenhead North), and the docks themselves - over half of Lee's fabrics were exported. There was a good supply of water for the dying process. There was also a plentiful supply of labour. Lee's employed largely women, not necessarily because they could be paid less than men, but because in this they were following the traditions of the cotton factories of Lancashire. For girls leaving school at 14 in those days, the range of jobs on offer was very narrow; domestic service, shop work, or Lever's soap factory at Port Sunlight. Lee's brought much needed work to not just the north end, but to Birkenhead as a whole, and at one time employed over 500 men and women.

In 1908 the north end of Birkenhead still had the atmosphere of a village. It was surrounded by farms, and lay beyond the end of the line of the trams. Bidston dock had not yet been built, and the Vacuum Oil Works (now Mobil), had only been open for a couple of years, on a very small scale. The Tapestry Works was built opposite to the Dock Cottages, said to be the first purpose-built flats in England, constructed in the 1840s to house dock labourers. Here too was the notorious pub known as 'The Blood Tub', the New Dock Hotel. Today, little remains of the old Birkenhead North, and much of its history is still to be written.

Chapter 2. A Tour of the Factory

What was it like to work at Lee's? Over the years faces came and went, new machines were bought, and new work practices introduced. Yet, in many ways life and work at Lee's remained very much the same in 1970 as it had been in 1908. The same skills were used to make similar products. Some designs were as popular in the 1960s as they were before the First World War. So let's go on a tour of the factory, following the making of the tapestries from start to finish; from the arrival of the undyed yarn in the dyehouse, to the packaging of the tapestries ready to be despatched to the customer.

The Dyehouse

> "...grimy men, bare of arm, hovering about great tanks of boiling, multi-coloured liquids...the atmosphere heavy and damp - almost choking for a time, until one got used to it."
> *Birkenhead Advertiser, March 18th, 1936*

With the wide varieties of colours in the tapestries and embroideries, it was essential that the firm had its own dyehouse. The dying was done in large vats or 'becks', which were filled with boiling water. The becks were of different sizes and designs for different kinds of yarn - wool, cotton, linen or silk. There were also machines to dye rolls of cloth. A spin dryer or 'whizz' and heated cupboards were used to dry the dyed yarn or cloth. Consequently, the atmosphere in the dyehouse was hot and very humid. As a dyer recalls:

> "It was a terrible job in the dyehouse. In the summer, you couldn't see the fella that was working opposite you - the

steam. In the winter, it was ordinary, it was alright. The
thing about the dyehouse was, a lot of people couldn't stand
that steam."

The dyers frequently complained about the atmosphere, and about the
ventilation equipment. These conditions largely explain why, after the
Second World War, so many workers stayed such a short time in the job.
Before the war, high unemployment forced the workers to accept the
conditions. Low pay was also a contributory factor, despite a
commitment by the firm from the 1920s to give the dyers trade union
rates. Dyers were paid a flat rate, and could earn little from overtime or
a complicated bonus scheme.

Dyeing was a job that could be learned fairly quickly, as a chemist was
employed to undertake the technical aspects of the work. The work
could be quite heavy, which may be why the management usually
employed male dyers. Dyeing was usually seen as a man's job in the
textile industry. Yet a few women did work in the dyehouse in the 1920s,
and also during the Second World War. Several women also did the job
after the war, particularly when they were short-handed. The women
proved themselves to be highly capable dyers:

> "The men across there were doing 10lb and 5lb jobs, and I
> was on a 200lb job. I said to the boss, 'I'm not getting a
> man's wage, you know'. He said 'Oh, I think you can do
> it better than them'. I said, 'That's not the thing though,
> is it...?!'".

The job had an element of danger, and minor accidents were not
uncommon. A variety of acids were used in dyeing, and caustic soda
was used in the mercerising process which turned cotton into imitation
silk. The management warned of the hazards of sulphuric acid in a
notice posted in the dyehouse in 1925:

> "This acid is exceedingly dangerous and utmost care must
> be exercised in handling it. A drop in the eye would

blind anyone for life. The least trace in clothing will
burn a hole...When anyone is measuring out sulphuric
acid or doing anything with it no-one may come within 3
feet of them...Anyone neglecting the above instructions
...will be liable to instant dismissal."

A dyer recalls the dangers involved in the use of acids:

"We had what we called the acid store, we had sulphuric
acid, all sorts of acid in there. If you spilt a tiny spot of
that it would bubble on the floor right away. It
wasn't a dangerous job, but it was dangerous stuff you
were working with. A friend of mine spilled it over her
foot, and she just simply swung over and shoved her
leg in a beck of cold water, it was the only thing you
could do...If you splashed it up in your face right away
you got blisters and sores."

There was one tragic accident when a man was killed when he fell into
one of the becks. For their safety, workers were provided with aprons,
clogs and thick rubber gloves, and a rubber overall was available for
particularly hazardous work. Yet it would be wrong to paint too gloomy
a picture of the dyehouse. If in summer "you had a cloud hanging over
you", in winter it was "nice and warm". Those who did not mind the
conditions enjoyed the work itself, and there was always good-natured
bonhomie among the dyers.

Card-cutting

A loom has thousands of threads known as 'warps' running from the
top to the bottom. To weave a piece of cloth, a 'weft' thread carried by a
shuttle goes from side to side across the loom, in between the warp
threads. Patterned cloth is woven on a more complicated loom called a
'jacquard'. The pattern is controlled by cards with holes punched in them
which are fed into the top of the loom.

Warp dyeing, 1930.

Before the cards could be punched with the right holes to produce a particular pattern, the artist's design for the tapestry had to be reproduced on graph paper, forming a mosaic of tiny squares painted different colours. Usually just one person was employed at Lee's as a card-cutter. He or she 'read' the pattern on each line of the graph paper, cutting out so many of a possible 576 holes on each card. Some designs needed as many as 15,000 cards, which were then laced together ready to be loaded at the top of the loom. Card-cutting was a job which required great powers of concentration, and there was no margin for error, but it was a rewarding one:

> "When they put that set of cards up on the loom, and I'd go in and see the weavers start the loom up, and I'd see the design coming out, it was incredible the satisfaction you got".

Weaving

What first struck the visitor or the new employee about the weaving shed was the terrific noise of the looms. As one weaver recalls, "You've never heard anything like it, you couldn't hear yourself speak! We used to lip read". Yet in other ways it hardly conformed to the image of a 'dark satanic mill'. The complex patterns and varied colours of the woven cloth meant that the room had to be bright, with a high glass roof and walls painted white to reflect the light. The work was divided between the sexes in the same way as in the Lancashire cotton mills: the maintenance staff or 'loom tacklers' were men, the weavers women. One weaver also recalls that Arthur Lee used to say that women made better weavers than men, because they had 'more patience and concentration'! Weaving at Lee's was a highly skilled job and school-leavers could not start on the looms straight away. Their first job was to wind the hanks of dyed yard onto bobbins, which were then fitted into the shuttles on the loom, as required. When the girls did start on the looms after two or three years, they worked alongside an experienced weaver. Yet this did not last for long, as they had been learning all the time. Each winder had several weavers to look after, and each weaver

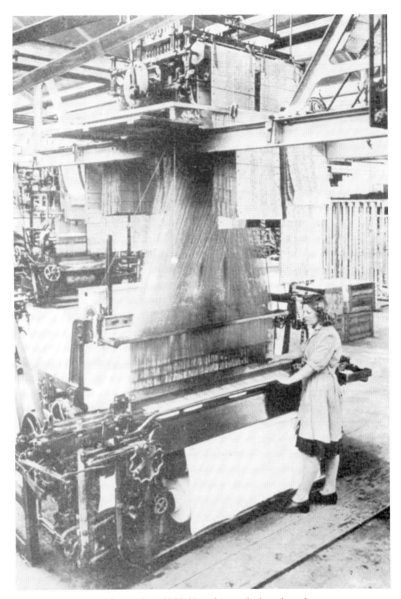

Weaver at a jacquard loom, about 1950. Note the punched cards at the top.

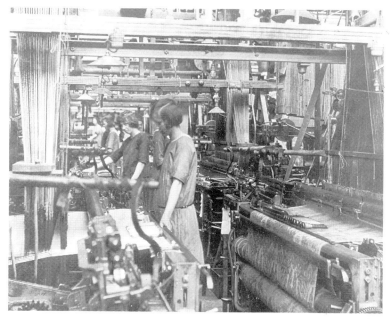

Weavers on the jacquard looms, 1920s.

would use a distinctive call when she wanted her winder to bring fresh bobbins over:

> "You'd collect all the bobbins and trip up to the loom with them. You would stay on that loom for about ten minutes, and she'd let you start it and stop it, and help you put ends in. By the time we came off the winding frame onto the looms, we'd had a pretty good grounding. The bosses knew this was going on, but didn't say anything, because that was what they wanted, a girl to show it to us. As long as you weren't wasting her time, she'd show you."

Weaving tapestry was certainly far more complex than weaving plain cotton:

"In Lancashire you look after 4 or 6 looms. We had one
weaver, one loom, because you couldn't possibly leave
ours. You couldn't take your eye off... because as soon
as you turned your back, something would happen.
When you're a jacquard weaver, even to the day you
left, something would happen in that tapestry that
you had never seen before. It was something different
every day."

Mr Armitage, the boss of the weaving shed, used to tell them that it
would take them five years to become a decent weaver.

Spotting any faults as rapidly as possible was essential, as weavers
were paid on piece rates. They were paid by the 'pick', a pick being
recorded on a counter at the side of the loom, each time one of the
shuttles went across. They were not paid at all while any faults in the
loom were being repaired, and lost bonus money if there were too many
faults in the cloth. Perhaps the worst thing that could happen to a weaver
was a 'smash', when the shuttle for some reason stayed in the middle of
the loom, breaking perhaps thousands of the warp threads: "You didn't
get a ha'penny pay while you were mending that smash ... and you'd be
nearly all day mending it." The wish to avoid any delays was taken to
great lengths by some:

"The old weavers would leave their loom on, and run like
the clappers to the toilet, and come back, and hope that it
was still alright, that nothing had happened."

Sometimes this was no laughing matter. On one occasion a weaver
was injured when, driven by the pressure of piece work, she left her
loom on while examining the underside of the cloth.

Wages were also affected by the length of orders that a weaver got:

"If you got a 60 yard order, you knew you were set for
that week, and your wage packet went up. But next week
you might be on little bits again. You never knew what
you were going to get on Friday."

Twisting the warp threads together by hand, 1922.

Short orders of perhaps just 2½ yards, known as 'fiddlers', were very unpopular, because when a piece was finished, there was often a long delay while the loom was prepared for the next. If the warp threads were coming to an end, all 5,760 of them were 'twisted' together by hand, and this took over two hours. In 1936 the firm bought a knotting machine which could do this in about half an hour. One or two women sometimes worked alongside the loom tacklers on these jobs, and also on the construction of the harnesses for the looms. The warp threads were prepared by women working on a warping mill, so that the threads were wrapped evenly and tightly on large rollers which could then be put into the back of the loom.

Sometimes the delays were so great that weavers would actually go home for the afternoon. Yet when their earnings were averaged out, between the wars at least the weavers were comparatively well paid. They were not only paid more than women employed in other jobs in the factory, they also earned more than the men in the dyehouse. In a good week, they would earn more than men in many other jobs:

> "If you had a long order, did a whole week on this one job,
> you could earn £3 a week. £3 a week was a lot, because in
> the thirties men at Laird's, their wage was under £3,
> about £2.15s. Men on the railway were getting just on
> £2 a week."

In the 1930s the men in the dyehouse complained to the management about earning less.

> "So they had a meeting in the canteen...Mr. Chris said
> 'If any of you men would like to be a weaver, and
> earn a weaver's money, you're quite welcome to go in and
> learn the job'. Not one man took it. We never heard any
> more about weavers getting better wages...They thought it
> was too hard, and too complicated!...They knew what we
> did, what the job was, but still at the same time they
> didn't think, because we were girls, we should get more

money than them... It was male prejudice. We just said 'yellow bellies'!"

The job certainly also had its unpleasant side. There were frequent accidents with the 2 foot long picking stick at the side of the loom, which was part of the mechanism which sent the shuttles across: "We had these picking sticks that come out, and if you put your hands near, you'd get a crack...It nearly paralysed you!" The shuttles themselves were a danger: "A shuttle would fly out and give somebody a crack on the head, but that was all in a day's work!" One weaver recalls being badly cut by a shuttle just above the eye, and a second time being knocked out completely: "It was just like somebody hitting you with a cricket bat." It could also be very cold in winter, the temperature once dropping to just 46°F. There was often a good deal of friction between the weavers and the maintenance men, and not for nothing was Jack Armitage known as 'the Red Terror from Upton'!

Yet generally the atmosphere was a friendly one. Despite the noise, "we used to all sing our heads off!" There was plenty of humour, too: "They used to play tricks on you when you first started ... send you for a bucket of steam, a left-handed screwdriver!" Nor could the job be described as monotonous, given the variety of pieces and the levels of concentration and skill required. Weavers enjoyed a feeling of independence:

> "You were given your order and your loom, and you were left to it. They were not there every minute to see. Only if you hit a snag did you shout for help. You had a job to do, and they trusted you to do it - and we did it."

With this level of independence, it was possible to take a pride in the finished tapestry:

> "You'd be finished, perhaps you'd done 60 yards of something beautiful for somewhere great, you'd be really thrilled ..... I did that!"

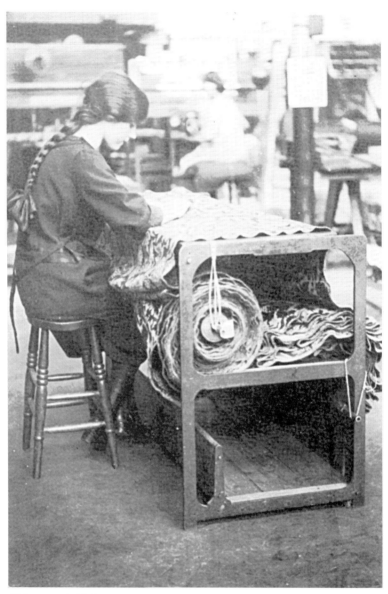

Picker at work, 1924.

The blockers were always women, and they had to be right-handed,because of the way in which the blocks had been cut. They stood in front of tables on which the woven tapestry was laid:

"In front of these girls stand trays of odd-shaped blocks and other trays of colours. Without a second's pause, ... they select a block, dip it on the pad of dye, apply it in exactly the right spot, and then with two or three substantial blows of a hammer or metal mallet carried in the other hand they stamp the impress, here, there and there, replace the blocks, take up another and repeat the process. So quickly do they work that there is scarcely any pause at all in the hammering".

Such was the impression of a visitor to the factory in 1938. Whole rolls of tapestry were blocked in this way. When a roll was finished it was put in a steamchest to dry.

Blockers at work.

A blocker certainly needed a good memory. Some pieces had as many as 940 different blocks, using 24 different colours! Before starting on a new pattern, the blockers had to carefully study blueprints which showed where each block went, and in which colour of dye. A blocker who began in 1912 recalls how she learned the job:

"I was put to work alongside another girl and the only training I had was to watch what she did and occasionally put on a block. It is the sort of job where you are learning all the time, and it was about three months before I was working on my own."

While the work was clearly highly skilled, it could also be quite physically demanding. On some of the thicker pieces of material, the blocks had to be struck with great force for the dye to leave an impression: "You had to have an arm like a navvy!" As tiredness led to a loss of production, from the 1920s the blockers were given two breaks or 'rest-pauses' in the morning, and two in the afternoon. Yet for one of the best blockers the firm ever had: "In spite of the breaks the day seemed very long and I was very tired at the end of it."

Conditions in the blockroom were initially far from perfect. The cold was a common source of complaint:

"At first the blockroom was part of the weaving shed, and it was cold and noisy. It was so cold the maul had to be warmed before starting work."

Even after the move to the new blockroom, the cold was still a problem: "In the winter those mauls would be like ice. Really cold." The maul was the hammer used to strike the blocks. A glove was provided to protect the blocker's left hand, but this was fingerless, since the blocks had to be very carefully positioned with this hand. Inevitably sometimes the maul would miss the block:

"You'd put the block on the material and you'd wham it.

That finger got more whams than the block! I was
always cutting that little finger."

The work was further complicated by the fact that not all the blocks
had to be struck at full force. Some were used only for finer shadings,
and these needed only a tap.

Blockers were paid by a complicated system of piece rates, based on
the number of blocks in each design, the size of the blocks, and the
colour of the background. The blockers did not always agree with the
way that each piece was priced. Many felt it was still possible to earn
more money on the easier pieces:

"You used to really dread going on a piece and seeing it had
23 boxes, you'd think 'I'll never make my money on that'.
If you got a little easy piece, well you are just sailing
through, you've only got to look at the pattern once and
you know how to do it .....I used to hate the
'Horseman', because it had that many fiddly bits to it. You
are talking about the saddle, stirrups, the soldier himself,
and the horse, and the background .... I hated that piece!"

The 'Horseman' required more than 500 blocks and 19 colours of wool
dye, involving over 1,000 applications for every yard of tapestry
produced. It was also one of the most popular designs ever produced by
the firm.

Another job in the department was the cutting of the blocks
themselves. This in itself was a highly skilled job. It could also be a
hazardous one. One block-cutter lost part of her finger while shaping
the blocks with a saw.

Colour-Mixing

The dyes used by the blockers were prepared in what was called the
colour room. Originally this department had been in its own room, but
in 1929 colour-mixing, blocking, braids and card-cutting were all

brought under one roof, in a new extension. About half a dozen women worked at the colour-mixing at any one time. While the dyes only came in three basic colours, red, yellow and blue, it was an often highly complex and time-consuming process to mix the exact colour needed

Storing rolls of blocked tapestry, 1920s.

for a particular pattern: "This could go on for a week, mixing a whole set of dyes, until you got it perfect."

The Embroidery Room

It was in 1910 that the firm first became interested in producing embroidery. Thorold Lee bought an antique piece of embroidery with the idea of producing a copy. It was soon found that there was a ready market for copies based on antique designs. At its peak, in 1930, over 120 women were employed in the embroidery department. Two different kinds of embroidery were carried out, and the embroiderers

Colour room, where dyes were prepared for use by the blockers.

tended to specialise in one of these. In needlework tapestry, the entire surface of a canvas material is eventually covered in stitches. This method was used at Lee's to produce carpets, wall-hangings and occasionally coverings for furniture. Crewel work is the kind of embroidery that most people are more familiar with, where the cloth is used as a background to the embroidered design. This method was used to produce curtains, and cushion and furniture covers.

Though this was highly skilled work, girls were set to work on embroidery on their first day:

> "I did hills for about a fortnight. I was looking green myself in the end! You used to start on them because it was an easy job, the hills ..... I was sick of hills!"

Yet as the embroiderer gained experience, so the interest of the job increased: "It didn't get monotonous because you were doing something different all the time...You didn't have the same design all the time."

Embroidery room, 1935, working on a panel for the ocean liner, The Strathmore.

The firm's publicity argued that embroidery "sometimes demands a considerable degree of artistic ability on the part of the girls." Those who worked on crewel embroidery were left to make some decisions on their own about colours and spacing. This was something that the management encouraged, as they felt that it gave an individuality to each piece that customers would appreciate.

> "Mr. Chris, one of the bosses, come round, explaining to some people. 'They're very unique these pieces', he said, 'because each girl has got different ideas on how to work and what colours to use. While they're doing one thing, they're planning another figure'...People liked to buy them because no-one else had the same you see, because different girls had done them."

However, for some crewel work, samples were made which even the most experienced embroiderer had to copy. Some seem to have preferred this: "It was less work for us because we didn't have to think as much, just copy it...It was easier, wasn't it?" Since the embroiderers worked on piece rates, having to think about their work and express themselves artistically, by slowing them down, could lose them money!

The embroidery room was spacious and light, with an all-glass roof. The cold seems to have been as much of a problem as it was in other departments:

"Sometimes it was very cold. They used to weave material in the weaving shed, and they used to give us the ends of the material to wrap round our legs."

In the summer there were other problems. In June 1927 the embroiderers asked the management:

"Could the fence outside the top door in the Embroidery Room be repaired to stop people from looking in, also could the rubbish (dead rats etc.) be moved as there is a terrible smell when the door is open in the summertime."

The embroideries were stretched out on frames on tables, and the embroiderers sat and worked with one hand under and one hand over the material. Sitting hunched over the work all day could cause backache, but the firm tried hard to provide comfortable seats. Yet, until 1935, the embroiderers had to provide their own scissors and thimbles. As eye strain was thought by the management to be the cause of slower production in the afternoon, at one time there were breaks every hour. A bell would be rung:

"Miss Aspey used to sit on her desk and we had to put our work down... and focus your eyes on the furthest object in the room. When you were on piece work you were a bit greedy, you wanted to do the work. She said to me, 'If that little girl in the brown dress doesn't put her work down, she will have to go home'!"

Embroiderers at work, 1928.

Particularly in the 1920s, when Alice Aspey was in charge, the room seemed to have the atmosphere of a school. The numbers employed were growing rapidly, and so most of the embroiderers were young girls who had just left school at fourteen. During one of the morning breaks the young girls did arm exercises in the works yard. Alice Aspey certainly seems to have been like a rather strict schoolmistress. When she entered the room:

> "The young ones would go quiet, they'd be a bit scared of her, but we'd got used to her, being there a couple of years... she was a right one, though! I never used to move out of the chair, except when I went to my lunch."

Those who worked well were rewarded as if they were still in school. On a chart on the wall in 1929 each embroiderer was given a coloured symbol each week depending on how she had worked. These ranged from dark red - 'much better than the average of last half year', to dark blue - 'a great deal worse', with the encouragement ' Make Yours All Red"! Another scheme offered them gold, silver and copper stars.

Yet the atmosphere did become more relaxed when Vincent Rockingham (nicknamed 'Rocky' by the workers!) became head of the department in the 1930s. As the firm's designer he could spend little time in the room overseeing the work. This was left to the four or five supervisors. From 1938 a radio was played for part of the day.

"We used to sing, tell jokes, and make up stories. It helped us along really, passed the time away, because you got that used to doing your embroidery, that you could do it nearly automatically. You wanted something to occupy your mind."

While most embroiderers seem to have found the job an enjoyable one, many felt that they were underpaid for what they did: "It was special work, it wasn't that it was a poor job, but they paid very poor wages." They were paid by a form of piece work, which for one embroiderer in the 1950s, took away much of the very real pleasure of the work: "I liked doing embroidery, but I didn't like the piece work, I didn't like having to rush it."

In the early years the wages clerk would come round every Wednesday with a ruler and a piece of cotton, and calculate as far as possible how many square inches of embroidery each worker had done, making allowance for the fineness of the stitches. Later the firm had charts made for each embroidery so that the piece rate was known in advance. Even so, like the blockers, many felt it was easier to earn on some pieces than others. And the embroiderers had to work hard to earn a decent wage:

"It was terrible sometimes. You had to rush like mad. Especially if you got a rotten piece. Some of the pieces weren't as good as the others to earn on. It

was a struggle to earn your wages. They had to make
your wages up to a certain amount, even if you didn't
earn them. If you got too much 'make-up' you had to go!"

In the 1920s at least, anyone who had 'make-up' for two consecutive
months faced the sack. For some it was a relief to go on a job like
ironing, for which a standard day wage was paid. Lee's also specialised
in the repair of antique tapestries, and work came from art galleries and
museums throughout the country. Again, many preferred to do this
work, as a good day wage was paid, and thus it was far less stressful.

Not all the women employed in the embroidery room actually worked
at embroidery. Usually two women worked at winding the wool. Others
worked on preparation of the designs, tracing them on to paper, and then
pricking out the outline with a needle. This was then placed over the
material and dusted with french chalk. When the paper was removed the
design could then be painted in with a fine brush. At one time about
eight young girls worked only at threading needles for the embroiderers,
to save them time.

In many ways the embroidery room was quite separate to the rest of
the factory: "We had our own door at the top end, we went straight out
into Stanley Road. We really didn't see very much of the rest of the
factory. We never went into it." There was also a feeling that embroidery
was 'a nicer class of work' than dyeing, weaving or blocking. Whatever
the reason, the embroiderers were sometimes seen as rather posh and
aloof by those in other departments. As a weaver recalls: "I think the
embroiderers thought we were common. They thought they were 'it' in
the embroidery room". As an embroiderer herself admits:

"Perhaps the girls themselves gave themselves a bit of an
air, the embroidery girls, so that's why the rest of the
works called us the 'Front Room Girls'".

Braids

The firm also came to specialise in the making of braids, ruches and tassels. These were decorative trimmings used on cushions or furniture coverings. In the 1920s only three or four women worked in this department, which was then in the embroidery room, but by the 1950s there were over twenty. At first they used small handlooms, which meant that the work could be quite heavy, but later some power-driven looms were developed.

The work itself was not too difficult to pick up, but it was important to get into a rhythm: "You had to get into the swing of it, because it had to be so very precise". They could help each other to keep time:

> "Eventually we got into it that good that we used to all work together, the four of us, all keep in time with one another, and sing, and keep weaving".

It helped to work in time to music on the radio, and Thorold Lee claimed that their production rate fell when the song 'Slow Boat to China' was a hit!

There were occupational hazards in this department also. On the ruching machine, for example: "When you first went on it, it cut all your fingers, with the warp that used to come through like a wire .... It was thin, very tight, like silk.". One thumbnail was always being damaged: "The nail used to catch all the time .... It was one of the hazards, there was nothing you could do about it, it used to break the nail".

Piece rates were paid here, at so much per yard. While more money could be earned on a 200 yard order, a few short orders kept the interest as workers here were expected to set up the looms themselves. This department was popular because of the variety of work - they also made ropes and cords used in interior furnishings.

The atmosphere was also a relaxed one: "You could go and have a little talk, nobody said anything, so long as you got your work done".

Artist at work in the studio, marking out a pattern for an embroidery.

Lack of space prevents us from doing justice to a variety of other jobs carried out around the factory. Some worked in the stores, some made up pattern books, and others prepared samples to be sent out to customers. Some worked on the packaging and despatching of the finished tapestries. Many of these jobs were carried out in the warehouse, under the supervision of Frank Hampson. It was also his job to grade the cloth first, second, or third class, which affected a weaver's wages. There were also a large number of office workers, administering personnel and welfare matters, and a complex system of sales around the world.

Workign on a hand ruche machine in the Braids department, 1936.

Chapter 3.
Early reminiscences, 1908 to 1918

For most factory workers before the First World War the working week was long and arduous and Lee's was no exception. In 1908 the hours at Lee's were the same as in the Lancashire cotton mills: 57 hours a week, with half an hour being worked before breakfast. However, the management soon became convinced that little work of any value was done in the first half hour, and so it was dropped. This they argued, "saved lighting and heating, and the workers were in better trim and better spirits". Before the First World War the last half hour for weavers was scrapped, and it was found that they did more work in the shorter hours. Yet the hours were still long. A blocker who began in 1912 worked from 8.00 am to 6.00 pm and also 8.00 am to 12 noon on Saturday morning, for which she at first got 4 shillings (20p) a week. Not all the workers lived in the north end of Birkenhead, and getting to work was not so easy, as a weaver who lived down by Argyle Street recalls:

> "There were no buses of course in those days, so I'd leave the house about quarter past seven every morning to be at work at 8 o'clock. I'd walk all that way up .... Sometimes if it was raining very heavy mother would give me a penny for the tram car, which dumped me at the depot in Laird Street, then I'd have to walk".

Conditions in the factory at this time were also quite primitive. At first there was no canteen:

"We used to take sandwiches, and we used to sit on the floor to eat them ... We stood on these loom boards to weave, and we sat on them to eat our lunch".

The sandwiches could be helped out by a halfpenny or penny portion of chips from the chip shop over the road in the Dock Cottages. Then Miss Walker, the head of the picking room started to make scouse for lunch at 3d a plate. However, this proved to be very unpopular, when it was discovered that it was made with black puddings! Soon after a canteen was opened, which proved to be much more popular. A piano was provided for the workers to make their own lunchtime entertainment. However, this was only after a notable incident which opened Arthur Lee's eyes to the conditions endured by his workers.

'Tea! Tea! Who gave you permission to make tea?!'

In these early days, the weavers were not even allowed to have a tea break in the morning. They had to work right through from 8.00 am to 12.30 pm. However, at about 10 o'clock, the boss of the weaving shed, Isaac Wilkinson, would go off to smoke his pipe. This was the opportunity to make an illicit cup of tea and have a sandwich. The weavers still had to watch out for Arthur Lee, so they could not use a tea pot. In those days jam came in brown earthenware two pound jars, and one of these jars was put at the side of each loom by the management filled with sand. The weavers occasionally had to throw sand between the belt and the wheel at the side of the loom, if these were failing to grip. So they made the tea in a corresponding jam jar. One day, however, a weaver recalls that Arthur Lee caught her making the tea in the picking room:

"I was holding it with my pinny, because the jar was hot, when I come face to face with Mr. Lee. He took his pince-nez off. He said he knew I was a weaver, he knew I didn't work in that picking shed, "What have you got there?" I was wishing the ground would have opened and swallowed me up. I said "Tea, Mr. Lee". "Tea! Tea! Who gave you permission to make tea? Get back to your loom! I put the tea down went back to my loom, and he ordered the boss, Ike, to kick the motor off, stopped all the looms and got us all in a bunch, all us girls, must have been around 16 or 17 of us. He was fuming.

At that time, songs were all the rage, and there was a song called 'How long has this been going on?' He said. "Tea! Tea! How long has this been going on?" Of course the girl behind me digged me in the ribs, because she was thinking of this song. We started smiling and he said "Don't you dare smile! You were the one that had the tea, explain yourself". So I thought, well, I'll tell him the truth, and nothing but the truth. So I said, "Well Mr Lee, I live downtown, and I have my breakfast at six or half past six of a morning, and I find that I'm hungry about ten o'clock". He said "Oh!, he hadn't thought of that". However, he ordered us to all get back to our looms, which we did.

The next day we were surprised when the office girl, Gertie Conway, brought this slip of typewritten paper: from such and such a date onwards, we are going to bring tea and cocoa round, which would be a penny or tuppence, and if you wanted a bun that was another penny. So we all had a bit of a conference, us lot, and said "It was cheaper to bring a sandwich from home and make our own tea as we had been doing, because that all comes out of our wages". I don't know what he said but we told her "Oh, he can keep his tea and cocoa!""

In contrast to the 1920s and 1930s, the management seem to have been rather ignorant about the working conditions of their employees at this time. A weaver remembers an accident when she fell off her bike on the way to work:

> "I was bleeding, my teeth had cut my lip, and I was in
> agony all that day. I had to go to the dentists after I'd got
> home from work, and he drew three teeth out at the front
> ... I was holding a handkerchief to my mouth all day at
> the loom, bleeding .... Nobody would take that much notice
> of you."

Yet at Christmas the workers were treated to a meal and a dance at the

Embroiderers relaxing in the Works yard, just after the First World War.

Blenheim Café in West Kirby. They could also enjoy a cheap holiday at Arthur Lee's holiday camp near Prestatyn. There were lighter moments at work too. When they had enough bobbins ready for the weavers, the young girls on winding taught each other how to dance behind the winding frame - until they were caught by Arthur Lee! The weavers from Warrington had also brought an old tradition of initiation with them:

> "I was on the winding frame, and you had to go round the looms, to get the empty bobbins. It was my first time round, and I was mesmerised by these looms ... Two of these women from Warrington got hold of me and shoved me under the loom. I got up and come out all covered with fluff and stuff! They said they did that to new girls".

All things considered, those who worked at Lee's before the First World War considered themselves fortunate:

> "We thought we were a lot better off than Lever's workers. They used to go to Lever's with a headscarf on, not a shawl exactly, but they never used to dress like we did. We had kid gloves on, and all that kind of thing! We

thought we were a cut above Lever's workers. You
were considered lucky if you were working at Lee's then".

The First World War

In August 1914, the whole of Europe was plunged into war. Many of
the men at the factory went off to fight, including Thorold and
Christopher Lee. While the Lees returned, at least two of the men from
the dyehouse lost their lives in the trenches. Yet at first there was little
effect on the business. After all, the war was 'going to be over by
Christmas'! As the war dragged on, so the orders fell away, and Arthur
Lee had to turn to alternative lines of business, such as the manufacture
of dolls. Eventually, women employees had to be told to look for jobs
elsewhere, though whether the factory closed altogether is unclear. The
firm invited along recruiting officers for the Women's Land Army and
the Women's Army Auxiliary Corps. Several joined the Land Army, and
others found jobs replacing men who had been called up.

Those women got their jobs back at the end of the war. But they were
shabbily treated in one respect on their return .Workers with five years
experience were entitled to a sum of money when they retired or left to
get married. However, when women came to leave after 1918, their
service before the war was not taken into consideration. A weaver who
left in 1920 was told there was no money for her by Jack Armitage, boss
of the weaving shed:

> "I was depending on that £50 to get things to get a
> home together...So I had a quick think and I said 'That's
> not fair'. He said 'No, I don't think so either, but that's the
> rule'. 'But what about the chaps', I said, 'who went to fight,
> and they've come back?' 'Oh, its different, it will still carry
> on for them'. So I said, 'That's not fair, I was doing my
> bit for King and country, same as the men were'. I said 'I'd
> like to tell Mr Lee that', but he was unapproachable...He
> went back to Mr Lee and explained, and you know what
> he sent me? £5, as a personal gift from him. I was very
> nearly going to go and throw it at him."

Chapter 4.
Between the Wars, 1918 to 1939

"Never before have we seen a textile factory of any type which can compete with Lee's for organisation."
British Association of Managers of Textile Works, 1934.

The inter-war years saw the tapestry works undergo great changes. A revolution took place in working conditions, welfare provision and relations between workers and directors. There were also changes in the production process itself. It was a time of innovation, new techniques, new markets and rising production levels. These were the halcyon days of ancestral homes, reproduction furniture and luxury ocean liners, a ready market for Lee's fabrics.

After the First World War the watchword in the industry was 'scientific management'. The organisation of the company's affairs, from long-term production planning to the smallest movement of the blocker's hand, was examined and measured in a never ending search for greater efficiency and production. The techniques of scientific management, with its concern for a 'fit and contented workforce', had a natural appeal to the Lees. For they themselves were in the tradition of paternal industrialists, like Lord Leverhulme in nearby Port Sunlight, who saw workers as human beings, not numbers, and had already begun to provide some facilities for their welfare. At the helm of the company now were Arthur Lee's two sons Christopher and Thorold. They divided their responsibilities between the 'psychological' and the 'mechanical'.

Thorold Lee (1881-1963) and Jack Armitage (right) in 1927.

Christopher developed a wide range of social and welfare facilities very advanced for their time. Thorold applied himself to the production of the tapestries as well as developing the kinds of fabrics the firm was known for in the 1920s and 1930s.

The story begins in 1920 when the Daily Mail held a '100% Efficiency Exhibition' in London, featuring the famous American efficiency expert, Frank Gilbreth. Gilbreth not only impressed the Lees but persuaded them to engage Robert Stelling, an industrial organiser from Scotland. Stelling, paid an initial £350 for his services, supplied the professional guidance the Lees were searching for:

> "Like all factories your problems classify themselves into two groups, the psychological and the mechanical."

Vocational Selection Test for blockers, 1920s.

In other words the company's future lay in the 'appliance of science', not only to how the tapestries were made but also to the people who made them. In the years that followed the factory was dramatically reorganised.

Scientific Management began even before the newcomer started work at Lees. As Christopher Lee once wrote:

"In 1925 we asked the National Institute of Industrial Psychology in London to prepare vocational selection tests for us because we were so worried about getting the right girls for the right jobs. They sent Miss Spielman...she spent a long time working at weaving, at embroidery, at blocking, actually doing the jobs, and then she worked out a set of tests."

Gladys Rimmer, who supervised the tests after the Second World War remembers that:

For blockers... I had to see if they could memorise where the colours went. And then there was discrimination of the shape. All the blocks were different shapes and there was a correct way of picking them up because they were marked for the thumb and the fingers. We used to take these out of the board and then ask them to place them in the correct position... that would show you if they were quick enough."

For weavers the capacity to 'think of several things at the same time' was valued. For embroiderers, a good sense of direction and nimble fingers. For the directors the tests were "...valuable not so much in picking out prospective star performers but in eliminating a certain number of unsuitable candidates".

However, as a small firm based in a tightly-knit community, Lee's could not choose its workers by such tests alone. It was very much a family firm, and generations of workers as well as directors followed each other into Lees. It was not unknown for four sisters to work side by side. A typical story is told by Gladys Rimmer:

> "I remember one kid - she had three sisters in already and she was the fourth. When one of her sisters was off she'd come and collect the wages on a Friday. She must have done this for a couple of years before she left school. 'I'm coming to work for you when I leave school.' 'Are you Joy?' I'd say. And every time she saw me she'd say it... The day she left school she was up there, 'I've come for my job' she said. Well, what could you do? We'd got three sisters. We asked her in. We found her a job."

Time and Motion

Applying the ideas of scientific management to the production process itself - the 'mechanical' aspect as Stelling called it - was far from easy. Making tapestries was hardly the same as making cars. There could be no production line. Henry Ford produced one make of car, the 'Model T' and, in his famous sales pitch, you could 'have any colour you want as long as it's black'. For Lees however, it was precisely the variety of colour and the wide range of designs, in orders of often only a few yards, that were its hallmark. Indeed, in embroidery, the initiative of each embroiderer in varying slightly each design was used as a selling point. Nevertheless, it was true that from the 1920s the firm was, in the words of Christopher Lee:

> "...convinced of the importance of studying all hand operations in minute detail in order to keep costs down to the lowest possible level."

After an intensive study of the blocking process used by Stelling, using special photographs as 'stereo-chrono-cyclographs', each blocker was taught the 'one best way to do blocking'. Each tiny movement the blocker made was reshaped to expend the least energy for the greatest effect. Individual boards were made, suited to the height of each

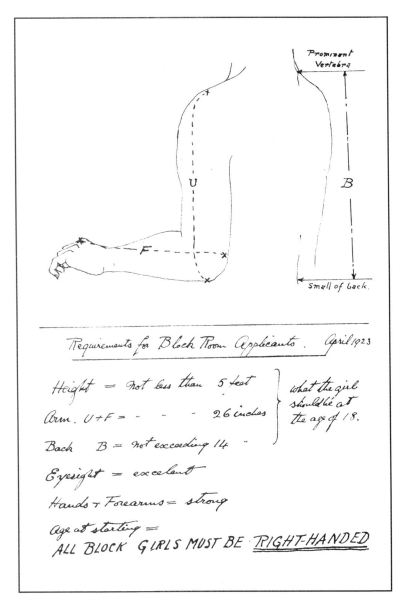

Guidelines to the Mutual Service Worker on the physical requirements of blockers, 1923.

blocker, so that her elbow matched the level of the table. The blocks were redesigned, making them easier, and so quicker, to handle. After Stelling had finished the production rate was almost 60% higher.

The scope for this form of work-study was limited however, and it was left to the incentive of piece-work to improve the output of most sections. Some observers were enthralled by this combination of creativity and organisation. S.B. Mais wrote enthusiastically, after visiting the factory in 1938, that:

> "...here in this factory I found science, art and industry blended more happily than I can remember ever to have seen anywhere else."

The workers, in the eyes of Mais, were "simple-minded and open-hearted...smiling and happy at their work". The reality however, of working by the piece, is not so simple:

> "It was hard going really. I used to get a migraine every month. I think it was the tension. I worked up until in the end I was actually sick from the migraine...the tension of trying to earn your wages."

Fatigue and Efficiency

During the nightmare of World War One the government had striven to produce ever-greater quantities of armaments, and was forced to study the 'efficiency' of the individual worker. In 1917 its Health Munitions Workers Committee declared:

> "The problem of scientific industrial management, dealing as it must with the human machine, is fundamentally a problem in industrial fatigue."

Though it is unlikely that they felt they were dealing with 'human machines', the Lees were already ahead of the government on this question, as Christopher Lee remembered:

Measuring up for a blockroom rest chair, 1924.

Young embroiderers exercising in the yard, 1928.

"It was before the war that we came across a book
by Josephine Goldmark entitled 'Fatigue and Efficiency'.
This set us thinking about the possibility of shortening
hours of work with a view to reducing fatigue at the end
of the day, and consequently improving fitness for work at
the beginning of the following day."

Indeed, when the last half-hour was cut from the working day,
production levels rose rather than fell.

Lee's had great trouble dealing with the increased demand for their
fabrics after the war. The blockroom, in particular, was a 'bottle-neck',
unable to keep pace with the speed of the weavers. Simply employing
more blockers was no solution in the short term for it took up to five
years to fully train them. So productivity was raised by two methods. As
we have seen a time and motion study was carried out under the
guidance of Stelling. Also the blockers were granted a break, or 'rest
pause' at 9.30 each morning,. This was not Stelling's idea, however, as
Christopher Lee recalled:

"It was noticed that Lizzie Williams... at half-past nine
would quietly stop work and take out a sandwich of bread
and butter and get down to a good second breakfast.
I mentioned this to the forewoman and she replied that she
was aware of it but didn't like to say anything to Lizzie, as
she was the best blocker that we had. I replied that if it
was good enough for Lizzie then I believed that it would
be good enough for the rest...The next day, on my
instructions, the department ceased work at half-past nine
and all the blockers went out to the canteen, where they
could sit down to enjoy any food they had and get a cup of
tea to go with it. This was very much appreciated
and definitely appeared to be helpful although no figures
are available."

A second 'rest pause' was introduced in the morning and another two in the afternoon. During this second pause the blocker would sit in a specially designed, adjustable 'rest chair'. Shortly the entire factory enjoyed such 'rest pauses'. As we have seen, rest pauses were, for a time, once an hour in the embroidery department, and the embroiderers were taken out into the yard for physical exercises. When the dyers began playing football during the rest pause the directors reminded the workers, in a notice pinned up in the dyehouse, what the purpose of the rest pause was:

> "Those employed on standing up and energetic work should sit down and rest, while those who have sitting down jobs can take light exercise. For the above reason those employed in the dyehouse must not play vigorous games during rest periods, but should take the greater part of the rest period sitting down quietly."

Soon a wide range of measures to safeguard the health of the workers was introduced. A 'Mutual Service Worker' was appointed, whose duties included first aid treatment, visiting employees at home if sick, and interviewing applicants for jobs. Medical inspections now took place 'as and when required' and dental care was compulsory. The firm even began a scheme, in the early 1920s remember, to pay for the services of an oculist and chiropodist. After 1922, when "parents of newly engaged girls complained of girls at work whose heads were not clean", all girls were examined for head-lice. In the inter-war years infectious diseases were massively more widespread than we know them today. The firm insisted that workers should stay away from work, with pay, if anyone at their home had any of the following diseases - Chicken Pox, Scarlet Fever, Diphtheria, Smallpox, Measles, Typhoid, Enteric Fever, Mumps, Plague, Pneumonia, Influenza, Cerebo-Spinal meningitis, relapsing fever and Cholera.

The Lee's worker who fell ill was certainly well looked after by the standards of the time. In 1922 a League of Help was established, funded by voluntary contributions from workers, an equivalent amount from the

directors and from the fines levied on those late for work. It was
controlled by a committee of two workers and two managers. Its stated
aim was to "help any workers placed in difficulties through illness or
misfortune by gifts of money, food, flowers, etc." and to "help such a
worker to make a complete recovery from the effects of the illness by
paying their expenses at the firm's Rest Home in North Wales." The
Rest Home was situated near Dyserth in the hills above Prestatyn. A
weaver remembers what happened to her when she contracted
pneumonia and was off work for nine weeks. Her experience is not
unusual:

> "I'd get bowls of fruit on a Friday. The welfare, Ida Macdonald,
> she'd come every Friday with my wages, have a little talk
> and see I was alright. When I was out of bed they sent me
> to camp (the Rest Home) for a fortnight."

Regular factory holidays were also an arm in the fight against fatigue.
Paid holidays, of course, were unusual in themselves in 1921. As late as
1938 the Ministry of Labour was still recommending that firms grant
one weeks holiday with pay. Even more unusual however, was the
regulation that those who were spending the week at a health resort, and
could prove it, received 11 days pay, while those who spent it at home
received only 5½ days pay. The directors made it clear that:

> "The objects of holiday pay are to encourage regular
> and punctual attendance at work and so ensure that girls
> shall be able to get away... and so get the greatest
> benefit possible."

Holiday pay could be reduced for those who were frequently late for
work. A weaver who started working at Lees in 1910 remembers:

> "We used to get off at Prestatyn and there used to be what
> you called the 'Coffee Pot' train from Prestatyn to
> Meliden. Then we had to walk. We slept in bell tents and
> you had to go to bed at eight or perhaps half-past eight.

'Now go on girls, get to bed' he'd (Arthur Lee) say, and fasten the tent up. We'd wait until all was quiet and we'd sneak out under the tent, go across the field, over the stile, and all the way to Prestatyn just to buy chips."

In later years bunks and huts replaced the bell tents:

"You just had two bunks, two blankets and a pillow, that was all, and a little ledge with a basin on it, and you went and got water, no running water or anything, very primitive really but they were comfortable, and we had fun. We were young, it didn't matter, living rough!"

Yet the girls still sneaked out to Prestatyn, only now it was for the 'last house' at the cinema.

Relaxing at the holiday camp at Dyserth, about 1930.

A Business Partnership

"We want you all to realise that the works is a big
complicated machine of which you are all parts. Even the
least prominent part is important and the machine cannot do
its work as well as it should do unless every part is
working smoothly without friction."
Foreword to a pamphlet issued to all workers, June 1924.

The Lee brothers sought to develop, if not a partnership with the
workers, then certainly a sense of belonging and a feeling of loyalty to
the firm. They did so not merely because of personal belief, though their
father's philanthropy and Quaker beliefs had clearly marked their own
characters. For the new age of scientific managers and efficiency
experts, the discontented, as much as the tired worker, was a poor
worker.

Partnership Certificates were issued to employees (or 'members' as
they were called from 1931) who, in the judgement of the director
"show genuine interest in their work and try to promote the prosperity
of the company". These 'shares' conferred no legal rights and had to be
returned on leaving the firm, but they fostered a sense of partnership
between the workers and the directors. The rarity of the pay-outs on the
'shares' had more to do with the economic fortunes of the company than
the intentions of the scheme's founders.

A Retiring Fund was established and those retiring because of ill
health, old age, or, in the case of women, marriage, received payments
depending on their length of service and the 'Quality of service
rendered'. Its object was "to encourage employees to give the firm a
large number of years of unbroken service." Those wishing to save with
the company for their retirement could do so with the Retirement
Savings Scheme, the firm acting as a Post Office or Savings Bank,
paying 5% interest. After 8 years unbroken service a form of
unemployment benefit was paid to those out of work due to lack of
orders, ensuring that, together with State benefits, they were receiving
three-quarters of their average weekly earnings.

All of this did not end with the 5 o' clock buzzer. If you wanted a book to read you could get it from the Works Library. The Friday night dance held in the canteen was a regular social item. The directors even tried to offer the land around the works as allotments. Between the wars it was true for many that:

Lee's Christmas Dinner 1936.

"We worked together and we played together. Our social life was very much based around Lees... apart from being a place where you worked it was a second home. Pa Army (Jack Armitage)... we were all 'his girls'. As he once told us: 'I know you call me Pa Army but I see more of you girls than your own father does'. We didn't work for them, we worked with them, which was different because you could go to them about any problem at all."

The Workers' Committee

Two years before the National Union of Textile Workers was created in 1922, a 'workers' committee' had been formed at the Tapestry Works consisting of elected representatives from each section of the factory. Its origins are unclear. Certainly, as a body set up by the management with a stated objective "to promote better mutual understanding between the workers and the management", it could be seen as just another arm in the drive for greater efficiency. Christopher Lee, certainly, listed its creation as one of the "steps towards scientific management". Yet it may not be so simple. According to one weaver, just before the Workers' Committee was formed a group of weavers had sent for and met trade union delegates from Blackburn. They had been prompted to write to them after discovering that a weaver could earn 35s (£1.75) per week in Blackburn, while 20 to 25s (£1 to £1.25) was more usual at Lee's. A committee room at the Comet Inn on Laird Street was booked and six rather apprehensive weavers met with two Blackburn delegates. Though no union was formed it may be that the Workers' Committee was established precisely to pre-empt one. It is interesting that the weavers' initial reaction to its formation was hostile. Management had to plead with the weavers to elect a representative to serve on it. And how did the Workers' Committee work?

> "We used to vote first. You'd have so many sections that
> would take part in the voting. People would put up. Then
> you represented that section that had sent you in. If they
> had any complaints they used to come to the member and
> we used to try to sort it out. Once a month we used to have
> a meeting in the canteen and all the complaints would
> be brought forward then, written into the book, discussed,
> and at the end of the meeting that book would be given to
> one of the directors..."

Were the directors opposed to unions, then, in this inter-war period? There are some who recall a hostility: "I believe somebody tried to get a union going, a man out of the dyehouse, and was told he was an 'agitator' and that's as far as it went". Another recalls: "Several times we tried to start a Trade Union but this was not well received by the management". The same worker remembers how the blockers staged a brief, and as far as we can tell, the only strike in Lee's history: "We sat on our tables and would not work until Mr Lee came to discuss the matter. Mr Lee did not appear but sent word that we could have a 4/ - rise...We were only on strike about two hours". This shows how highly skilled the blockers were and what power this gave them if they chose to use it.

However, in November 1939, a special notice was posted up which read:

"...it seems that some members believe that the directors object to their joining trade unions. This is entirely incorrect. The directors have no objection whatever, and in fact they feel that from some points of view it would be advantageous if our members joined trade unions. They have no wish to bring pressure to bear in either direction and sincerely hope that all concerned will take the same view and leave each member to decide for himself. This applies to women as well as men."

It might be said that the timing of this notice - weeks into the Second World War - was not accidental. The wartime role of the unions was to organise increased production and many formerly hostile employers welcomed them. A more likely explanation for the lack of a union however, is the nature of the firm itself. Small, intimate, family-based, Lee's was isolated from the great textile centres of Yorkshire and Lancashire. As one worker remembers:

"We knew everybody by name. 'T.D.' (Thorold Dracup Lee) knew us all. Conditions were very good. The money was as good as anywhere else. No-one was breathing down your neck all the time. The books were open to the Workers' Committee if they wanted to see them."

For one 'tackler' it was the fact that brothers and sisters worked side by side in the factory that would have made the union rule-book and 'demarcation' unpopular. "A brother doesn't say to a brother... you don't do that because I do it". The exceptional family atmosphere, remarked on by almost all the ex-workers spoken to is important in this respect:

> "And the bosses. I mean you don't find bosses these
> days mixing in with you and doing the same work that
> you're doing. They'd tell you what to do and you had to do
> it but they mucked in. Tony Lee used to come in the
> dyehouse and dye yarn. Used to go on the looms and
> weave with the girls. He went in every department.
> Fantastic!"

The family atmosphere was undoubtedly an important factor in the acceptance of relatively low wages:

> "I still think we were underpaid for what we did. When
> you think of it! But it was a family firm, and they did look
> after us..."

Whatever the reason, the Workers' Committee was the forum in which, from 1920 onwards, workers and management argued out their different interests. For if the slump of the 1920s and 1930s proved anything at all, it was that neither philanthropy nor scientific management were any match for a world slump in trade. Wage cuts and lay-offs soon followed and the Workers' Committee felt that they could not oppose them.

Boon and Slump

Michael Lee has recalled the firm's fortunes during the inter-war years:

> "The 1920s, up to the 1929 crash, seems generally to have
> been a period of prosperity and expansion. The depression
> of the early 1930s brought hard times. I remember my
> father saying that his income was reduced to a third of what
> it had been in the 1920s. People used to work one week on
> and one week off so that they had one week's wages and
> one week's dole in a fortnight. This was at a time of which
> it has been said 'If you were unemployed you could starve'."

In the two years from 1930 to 1932 unemployment doubled in Birkenhead until one in three were out of work. At Cammell Laird the shipbuilders, the labour force was decimated, falling from 6000 to around 2500. One North-ender, a weaver at Lee's, recalled those times:

> "I remember the rail lines to the docks would be rusty like they are now, and crowds would gather on the corner, perhaps rolling a cig... men would walk their whippets to Moreton Common for something to do. At Lee's most girls had fathers or brothers in shipbuilding, so they were hit hard. So they asked us 'Whose father works in shipping?' If yours did you got the work - 3 (weeks) on 1 off. If not, you didn't - 2 on 2 off. I was the breadwinner."

Many teenage girls at the Tapestry works found their wages making all the difference to the family budget. "My father was out of work, so it made a big difference". A weaver remembers that: "When you got back and we had a good week you'd put some by to help you through the next couple of weeks". Obviously having a wage that fluctuated from one week to another could be a stressful experience in the depression.

Birkenhead saw fierce battles between the unemployed and the police around Price Street in September 1932, as mounting protests against the means test and pitifully low levels of benefit erupted into violence. The unemployed demanded an end to the degrading means test and a 2/ - (10p) increase in the relief payment for adults. This would take the payments, for a man, to 15s 3d (76p) and for a woman to 13s 6d (671/2p). The Birkenhead News called their demands 'arrogant'. The chair of the Health Committee meanwhile was out to make further savings: "The trouble is that the blind are not blind. I do not wish to be flippant but I myself have seen one of these so-called blind persons playing nap". It was just this official contempt that sparked the riots of 1932. The increased rate was eventually won.

At Lee's the Workers Committee demanded of the management "not a big wage but a living wage". Many were forced to work short time or be laid-off all together. In 1930 there were 119 embroiderers. By 1934 there were less than half that number. Those under 16 had to attend the 'Dole School' as the Beechcroft settlement in Whetstone Lane was called:

> "You had to go there for the three days that you were off. It was like a school. You went and you did English or Maths or whatever for three days. If you didn't go there you didn't get your dole."

One woman remembers she signed on for so long that her mother became convinced that she had been sacked and wasn't 'letting on'. Some took up dressmaking to make up their lost income. Some, the youngest, were content to "wander round Grange Road, trying the hats on". At the dole office itself, on Bridge Street, the Lee's workers seemed to receive preferential treatment with a special window set aside for them:

> "When we went down to sign on at the Labour Exchange you'd see some of the clerks nudging one another and saying 'Be careful what you say, they're from Lee's'".

Lee's and the North-End

When the works finally closed in 1970 one local newspaper commented on the "tragic" demise of "a firm which has been part of the pattern of life in Birkenhead for almost all of this century". More so than at any other time was this true of the inter-war years. Lee's was indeed part of the 'pattern of life' in the area. Think of it from a child's point of view. For a child living in the North-end of Birkenhead Lee's Tapestry Works was a very important place indeed. Above all it provided one of the few escape routes to the countryside. When Arthur Lee came to Birkenhead he founded a children's holiday camp at Dyserth in North Wales and another near Ruthin. Each year, "between three and five thousand children are taken to Dyserth at the modest sum of ten shillings a week for board and lodgings. Children who live in the borough are allowed special preferential rates" noted the Birkenhead

Young Lee's workers with poor children at the holiday camp at Dyserth, 1931.

News in 1932. Poor children, many from Charles Thompson's Mission on Hemingford Street, Birkenhead, could escape to the countryside for a few fleeting weeks to enjoy the country air, sports, swimming, walking and climbing. "We had collection boxes" recalls one worker, "that went round the works and all through the years it helped to pay for this free holiday for the children. Very often they'd come back with a new pair of shoes each."

The camp and the children were looked after by a full-time warden and by the tapestry workers themselves. They would fix the camp up each year ready for the March opening.

A weaver remembers:

"He'd say 'would any girl like a week in camp?' We didn't get paid for going but we were kept and we had a holiday, we enjoyed it as much as the kids. We used to volunteer and go with them to look after the kids, take them out

60

rambling over the mountains so they wouldn't get lost...
Some of them were little terrors but we had a free hand,
"Hey, now don't do that again". Sixteen and you were
bossing little kids around, it was great. Because I had
three brothers who bossed me, I got my own back..."

Come Christmas time:

"There was a big tree and all the kids got a toy off it.
They'd get an orange or an apple. The girls used to make
dolls for it and dress them. So many of the poorer ones
would get a food parcel."

On a Wednesday night, all year round, would be Arthur H. Lee's Magic
Lantern (Slide) show:

"He used to give it to the kids from the Dock Cottages,
there'd be anything up to about 50 of them, all piled in. He
used to have a theme song and the words used to flash up
on the screen as somebody played the piano - 'Courage,
brother do not stumble, though the path be dark as night'
...the kids used to sing at the top of their voices as soon as
it started."

Of course it was not always so easy:

"He used to stand in front and try to lecture them... and
of course they were an unruly gang of kids, they used to
shout and bawl and he'd get really mad with them, and it
would all end up in chaos and they'd all be turfed out."

A child in need of a hot meal could often find one if he or she hung
around the works canteen.

Arthur Lee, the firm's founder, died in 1932, aged 79. The Birkenhead
News wrote an obituary headed, simply 'A Friend of Poor Children'. He

was cremated and his ashes scattered over the hills near the holiday camp at Dyserth.

Women, Work and Marriage

Before the Second World War, women normally left full-time paid work when they got married. It was generally felt that a husband's wage should be enough to support a wife and family. It was practically a social disgrace for a man if his wife continued to go out to work. A married woman's place was in the home, bringing up a family. At Lee's, it was a rule that women had to leave when they got married. Perhaps this was because the management felt that it was unfair for a married woman to deprive a single woman of a job: "It was the rule they worked. Once you married, I suppose they thought one pay packet was enough". However, it seems it had more to do with the level of skill in a job like weaving:

> "You had to leave when you got married, because if you were having babies, they couldn't afford to suddenly lose a weaver, and nobody taking your place. So when you were engaged, they got another girl on learning, so that when you leave there's somebody to take your place."

It was easier to time a marriage than a pregnancy! In those days there was no question of having a nursery so that women with children could continue in factory work. As it took time to train a new weaver, for example, in the 1930s the firm offered a 'Long Notice Bonus'. Women with five years service or more received £1 if they gave six month's notice of leaving to get married, ten shillings (50p) for three months. The firm also offered an incentive for women to delay their marriages as far as possible. In the 1930s they received £10 for each year after 8 years with the firm, up to a maximum of £150, on leaving.

For some Lee's women, there was no question of wanting to work after marriage: "I don't know whether it was a rule or not. I never thought about working after I was married, so it didn't occur to me". Other women desperately wanted to stay at work, to the point where one woman wore her wedding ring on a chain around her neck. When it was

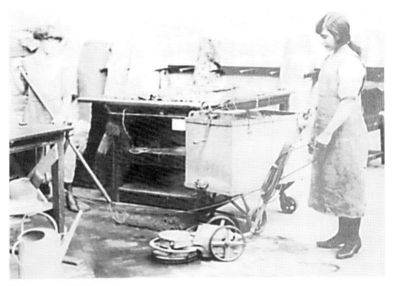

Cleaning up, 1924.

discovered that a woman in the embroidery room was married, she was immediately sacked, and lost all the money that she would have been entitled to on leaving to get married. These women may have wished to stay because they enjoyed the work; more likely it was an economic necessity. Very often a husband's earnings were not enough to support a wife or a family, whether through low pay, unemployment, or the irregularity of earnings on the docks, for example. The irony was that though they had 'officially' left paid work, many married women still had to do irregular and casual work such as charring, and homeworking of many kinds, to make ends meet. This was on top of the full-time, unpaid job of looking after a home and a family.

At Lee's, as in the country as a whole, it was the war that changed the entrenched attitudes about married women and work. As one weaver recalls:

> "I was the first one that didn't leave. I got married in August, (1939), and the war broke out, so I just automatically stayed on - they didn't sack me."

Chapter 5.
'Khaki and Canvas': Lee's during the Second World War, 1939 to 1945

In September 1938, the firm organised a trip by train to a Trade Fair in Glasgow, and over 200 of the workers went:

> "When we were coming back, there were rumours of war. Somebody said that we'd all have to get out of the train, and all these silly rumours. But we got home alright."

This was at the time of the 'Munich crisis', when Hitler was threatening to invade Czechoslovakia. During the crisis 38 million gas masks were issued to every man, woman and child in the country, and hasty preparations were made in case the Germans launched a massive air attack. On September 27th an official from the Air Raid Precautions services (ARP) visited the factory, to explain what could be done in the event of war. On September 30th, Prime Minister Neville Chamberlain sold out the Czechs to Hitler in return for a piece of paper which secured 'peace for our time'.

But war seemed inevitable, and the preparations continued. In January 1939 a meeting was held in the canteen for male employees interested in going away for 15 days military training under the National Service scheme. In July 1939, the firm announced that female employees who joined up for National Service in the event of war would keep their years of service regarding retirement benefits, if they returned when the war was over - a contrast to what happened in the First World War! At the same time, sirens were fitted in the works, and one in ten of the workforce were being trained by ARP officials. On September 1st German troops moved into Poland. A notice was put up in the works: "From tomorrow, 2nd September, and until further notice, every Works member should bring his or her respirator (gas-mask) to work". During working hours on September 2nd a practice evacuation into the air raid shelter beneath the colour-mixing and block room was held. On the following day, September 3rd, at 11am, Chamberlain's ultimatum to Hitler had expired, and war had begun.

Going down to the Air Raid Shelter at Lee's during the Second World War.

At first the management thought that after an initial fall in business, orders would pick up again, judging by what had happened in 1914. As the younger male workers could now be called up at any time, the directors hoped that most of the women would stay on. The firm made a loss of £1,100 in the first two months of the war, but there was no recovery in business. Short-time working had to be introduced, at one time one week on, and one week off. As a result, many women began to look for work elsewhere, the firm doing its best to help them find situations. With so many men being called up, jobs were not too hard to come by. Many found work at a munitions factory in Aintree, others at ICI in Runcorn, others cleaning and repairing aircraft at Hooton. Others simply left as they got married. Some replaced men in the dyehouse who had been called up, doing the same job for less pay! Business continued to fall away, and by 1941 the embroidery room had been taken over by another firm, Alcock's, for essential war work connected with parachutes and barrage balloons.

'Khaki and Canvas'

By this time, however, the management had secured contracts for Government work. By September 1940 five of the jacquard looms had been converted to weave khaki and canvas for the army. The braid looms were also converted to make webbing for rucksacks. In helping the war effort and keeping the factory going in this way, the directors were also looking to the future:

> "Some day the War will be over and we shall want to go
> back to our old type of business of supplying the world
> with the most beautiful upholstery fabrics that are
> woven anywhere, and for this we shall want weavers who
> have been kept in training and have not forgotten their skill."

The dyeing and weaving of khaki and canvas was felt to be a rather routine and dull job compared to making tapestries. When the khaki was woven it also gave off a white dust which was a health risk:

> "It was so dusty, you started brushing up at one end of the
> aisle and before you got to the other it was back again. It
> was incredible... That's why I left in the end, because of
> the dust. It was getting on my chest."

The working week was also increased to help the war effort, from 44 hours to 52 per week, from 7.30am to 5.30pm, with only half an hour for lunch. The weavers and mechanics had to work on Boxing Day 1940, as the firm was behind with the delivery of two Government contracts. Nearly everyone willingly accepted the sacrifices that had to be made: "If we saw a job that wanted doing, we did it". However, in August 1940 it was reported that splints, bandages and aspirins had been stolen from the factory's First Aid boxes.

'The Phoney War'

After a few weeks of the war, the fears of massive air raids or gas attacks by the Germans were receding. On September 18th 1939 the management had to put out a reminder that gas masks had to be brought to work. Anyone who forgot was sent home to get it. Two men and four women workers stayed in the factory each night on fire-watching duty, beds and a breakfast in the staff dining room being provided. In September 1940 the directors announced a plan, as at other factories, to work through the air raids as far as possible. Spotters on the roof were to warn when it was absolutely necessary to take cover. Workers could, however, take cover as soon as the official sirens sounded.

Lee's workers made a big contribution to the war effort outside the factory also, on ARP and other duties. Some, for example, joined the Women's Home Guard:

> "We had to learn how to use a rifle, to clean a rifle, combat, march, and throw hand grenades, drill, all sorts of things."

Birkenhead's Blitz

By September 1940, Birkenhead's 'phoney war' was over. The town was bombed eleven times in that month, and the raids increased in severity until after Christmas. On the single worst night of bombing, March 12th 1941, over 200 people were killed. Altogether the raids on Birkenhead took the lives of 464 people. Over 2,000 houses were completely destroyed, and two out of every three houses in the town were damaged.

Fire squad shelter at Lee's, November 1939.

Lee's was fortunate not to be directly hit, at any time. The Vacuum Oil Works down by the docks, just a few hundred yards away, was set alight by incendiary bombs on the night of March 12th, 1941, and almost completely destroyed. Occasionally the workers did have to go to the underground shelter, and the factory was evacuated when a sea mine landed nearby:

> "We were all working away there, and somebody said
> 'Stop your loom, all clear off out, quick!' - an
> unexploded bomb in the back where the allotments were."

Families in nearby houses were also evacuated and spent the night in Tollemache Road School, until the mine was defused. On another occasion, a nearby blast smashed much of the glass roof in the weaving shed, but fortunately the looms were not badly damaged.

'Worker's Playtime'

Life at Lee's in the war was not all hard work. ENSA (Entertainments National Service Association) concerts were regularly held in the canteen, to keep up morale. From 1942 the American servicemen around the docks were a welcome diversion for the young women at Lee's: We were American mad, you've no idea. The pictures we used to go and see, the uniforms, everything. Anyone to do with America was just terrific!" As well as bringing romance into many women's lives, the Americans were a source of wartime luxuries, such as chocolate, cigarettes and nylons! The young weavers used to seek them out during their lunch hour: "We used to play ball with them at lunchtime. Down Stanley Road, there's the Penny Bridge. There was an American ship in at the time. We went down to see if we could see any Americans... So we played football with them on the quayside".

The American connection of the firm also helped morale in the war. Workers in Lee's sales offices and showrooms across America sent food parcels at Christmas to the Birkenhead workers.

Chapter 6.
'In a World of Mass Production', 1945 to 1970

The first problem to be faced after the victory celebrations were over was straightforward enough; how to get the factory going again. The war scattered the highly skilled workforce of 1939 and wreaked physical damage on the plant and equipment. Weaving canvas and khaki had left the looms in poor condition.

The war undoubtedly changed many things. The first pre-war rule to go was that which had forbade married women to continue working at Lees. The reason is obvious. Many pre-war workers were now married. Others had left all together. Either the rule was dropped or the looms stayed silent, the blocking tables unused:

> "After the war they wanted any weaver available - 'Come make up a day between you, anything, just come!' - so we all went, we rallied."

Many weavers remember vividly their return at the War's end:

> "Pa Army kissed us, hugged us, fell on our necks. 'Oh, Thank Goodness!', he said, 'Come on through'. We went through into the weaving shed and some of them were going alright. Loom 13 was a double-header. We got up to 13 and I looked at it and I went 'Ah, Ah', nothing on this at all, no warps, no binders, nothing, just standing there. He said 'Jess, this is your loom'. 'It was', I said. He said 'It will be again now!'."

It was a great struggle though, to get the works moving again:

"... most of the harnesses in the loom, which is made up of linen thread dipped in oil, were more or less ruined. When they went to use a set of cards again, they'd been left in a certain area of the works where, with the bombs and the kids throwing bricks most of the glass in the roof had been damaged and the rain had got on them.
So sometimes, when they went to pick a set of cards, they fell to pieces... literally. And out of all this chaos, it came back, gradually, to what it originally was. As you got one loom weaving it was an achievement."

In many ways, however, it was not 'business as usual'. The rest homes had been sold off. The League of Help and the Savings Schemes now seemed quaint rather than innovative as personal savings were covered by post offices and building societies. The old vocational selection tests seemed to have been, for a time at least, inoperable:

"It all broke down because in full employment the girls won't wait; they expect to be taken on straight away. If they are asked to come back again for a test they get a job somewhere else."

Attracting, and retaining workers remained a problem throughout the post-war years. Many chose Levers at Port Sunlight in preference to Lee's: "If there had been more money I probably would have stayed. I was on £2.12s a week when I started there (1958). Two and a half years later I was only getting £3 and I left and went to work at Levers and I was on £8 ..."

Stephen Lee, in charge of the embroidery department, penned a worried note to his brothers in 1954: "To summarise: fewer girls remain to become 'old girls'. Old girls have experience and are the backbone of planning. Any business needs bones".

Presentation of certificates and commemoration gifts to workers with over 25 years service, 1956.
Back Row: Emily Joinson, May Judge, Lora Fairclough, Wilf Armitage, Nora Shaw, Lilly Stanley, Violet Gaunt, Tony Horner, Zaidie Clarke.
Middle Row: George Broomby, Dorothy Sadler, Phyllis Hardy, Mona Smith, Vera Waring, Mr. Tarbutt, Leslie le Fevure, Jack Armitage, William Sadler, Robert Cottam.
Bottom Row: May Smith, Elsie Shakeshaft,May Wild, Florry Roberts, Thorold Lee, Christoper Lee, Alf Hayes, Gladys Rimmer, Dorothy Blythe.

The post-war world was a precarious one for a small, specialist firm like Lee's. The instant and the disposable were in vogue, not the quality and durability Lee's offered. The reproduction furniture market had gone and the luxury liner, an important market for Lee's, began to be replaced by the aeroplane. Furniture was increasingly being covered in mass produced plain fabrics. In the 1950s the British Productivity Council noted the problems this posed to Lee's:

"... most of the work must be done by hand and...
even moderately sized orders are rare. Thus 940
different colour blocks are used in one particular design...
while 10 to 15 yards is a typical length for weaving
orders, compared with many thousand yards in many
textile mills."

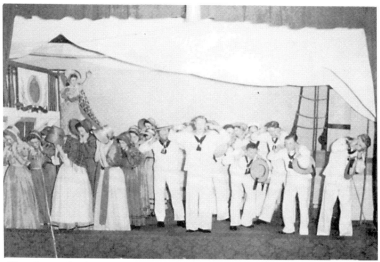

After the war Stephen Lee organised the 'Tapestry Players', works members who would stage a play or a musical every year. Here we see a scene from Gilbert and Sullivan's H.M.S Pinafore.

Christmas Party, 1950.

In 1958 the firm celebrated its 70th anniversary with an exhibition at the Williamson Art Gallery. The mood was confident: "While practising an ancient craft it has always been our policy to use the most modern methods, whether technical or managerial, which can be applied to our kind of business." They aimed to, "make cloth better and more beautiful than ever before".

Certainly the mid-1950s saw a full order book and an export trade in 19 countries. Lee's were almost as well known overseas as in Britain. One story, told by Peter Lee, highlights this only too well. It concerns a Canon from Liverpool Cathedral who was anxious to buy a suitable cloth for cassocks:

> "He went to Italy to buy cloth and went into a shop in
> Milan. He saw a fabric that was just right and asked
> 'Where can I get that fabric?' 'Well' they said, 'there
> is a company in Birkenhead called Arthur H. Lee and Sons...'"

There were certainly many 'prestige orders' in this period. Jackie Kennedy used Lee's fabrics to decorate the White House. Harold Wilson's No.10 Downing Street also used materials from Lee's. The Sheik of Kuwait ordered an embroidered wall hanging constituting 1,200,000 petit-point stitches. Indeed, in December 1968 Peter Lee felt it necessary to tell the public, perhaps rather optimistically given the price of Lee fabrics, that: "We don't just sell to the palaces, castles and mansions. Our products can be found in ordinary homes too."

The sixties, however, were a constant battle by the company against its own disadvantages of size, a craft-based production process and, ironically enough, its reputation. Synonymous with high quality yet expensive material:

> "Every time we tried to reduce the fabric to a more
> commercial price; as soon as we produced anything
> ordinary, it never worked. People did not expect that of
> us. Back to the champagne and caviar. That's what
> they expected of us."

Various attempts were made to increase sales. A tapestry weave was developed which could stimulate crewel embroidery but could be sold at a lower price on a regular yardage. In 1965 new high-speed German

Factory guides, 1951.

looms were bought as part of an overall efficiency drive involving a new 'image', new lines of printed linen and chintzes and new marketing methods. In 1967 they tried to break into the markets of theatre furnishings and aircraft upholstery. In 1968 many workers put in unpaid overtime as part of the 'I'm Backing Britain' campaign, the national drive to buy 'British goods'. Ironically about one in two of the firm's own tapestries were sent abroad!

But it was all to no avail. The problem was a simple one. Mass produced fabrics of a plain design were becoming standard. Lee's had one chance for survival. As Christopher Lee put it, in 1967:

> I have the impression that, in a world of mass
> production where the exclusive is becoming ever harder to
> find there will continue to be a place, even if it is only a
> small one, for craftsmanship and beauty which are not mass
> produced."

Closure

It was not to be. In 1970 Tony Lee was forced to admit:

> "Our problem is that craftsmanship tends to be going
> back to being a cottage industry. Unfortunately, we are
> neither small enough nor big enough to compete. The
> only thing that can save our firm now is a takeover."

The takeover never came. The closure was announced to the workers on 31st July 1970. Their reaction was a mixture of anger and sadness. As one weaver put it: "The bottom fell out of your world after 42½ years..." For Mr. Tony Horner "The country must answer for it if we go under. Nobody in the world can do the work we turn out here". For another worker, "This was a job a man could take pride in. I suppose I shall end up in a factory pushing something into a conveyor belt". Workers received little in redundancy pay:

> "We got about £300. Chicken feed isn't it? Well, you see,
> our wages weren't very much that's why. I'd been there
> 42 years but they only went back the last 20... and we were
> only getting about £12 a week."

For the press Lee's represented a "victim of the age of automation". Sixteen years on it is still a bitter memory for many:

> "To me it was a tragedy, for the firm, for the girls,
> because it was unique. It was a place on its own. There was
> not another one like it and Birkenhead should be ashamed
> for letting it happen... but for me as long as there's a weaver,

an embroideress, a blocker left, the tapestry works
won't die, because whenever we're together... we're back."

On December 2nd machinery and plant were auctioned off and the
unsold looms were broken up for scrap. Some of the buildings were

*Emily Reid putting in the last stitch of embroidery before the closure of the factory in 1970.
Looking on from left to right are: Michael, Peter, Tony, Christopher ad Stephen Lee.*

demolished and others used to build a supermarket which remains
today:

"I often think I'm going back to work now when I
go to Kwiksave. When you go through the main entrance
it's just like walking into the stores and then through to
the weaving shed."

The Williamson Art Gallery preserved a wide selection of tools,
materials, photographs and archives from the works and created an
exhibition of the workers' achievements. It has been by digging deep
into those archives as well as talking to the participants that this history
has been constructed. Perhaps this one document in particular, a letter

from the Works Committee to the directors on the closure of the firm in 1970, gives an insight into the Tapestry Works.

ARTHUR H. LEE & SONS LTD

The Tapestry Works

4th August 1970

The Works Committee expresses the sympathy of all works members to the Directors for all their strenuous efforts during the last five years to keep the factory going. As members we naturally feel heartbroken that the family atmosphere is going to end, and also the fact that the world at large should show so little concern for the sheer craftsmanship that has prevailed here for the past eighty years. We would, however, like you to know that we are very grateful for everything you have done. We are proud that we, with your help, backed Britain but are sorry that no-one backed Lees Fabrics. We have no regrets and would wish the Directors all the best in the future in the knowledge that we have left our mark in the fabric world and can safely say that we are second to none.

The Works Committee

Epilogue

The community spirit fostered around Lee's Tapestry Works continues to grow in the North End of Birkenhead today.

Since 2001, new work has been taking place to develop the green space called Ilchester Square in front of St. James' Church. Groundwork Wirral carried out an inclusive community consultation about what local people would like to see happen to Ilchester Square in the future. This involved working in partnership with the North Birkenhead Neighbourhood Forum, local agencies, Wirral Metropolitan Borough Council and various community, tenants and residents groups to organise a community fun day in September 2001. Barclays Site Savers, Wirral Waterfront SRB6, Sure Star and Wirral CVS funded the project. Groundwork Wirral staff gave out questionnaires and a landscape architect was available at the event to talk about ideas. An artist worked with children on collages to express their ideas for the green space.

The arts consultation continued, including work at Portland Primary School. An artist worked with children to make a school collage to illustrate what the children would like to see growing on Ilchester Square. Groundwork Wirral also worked with local Parents and Toddlers groups, talking to parents and guardians about the project while children worked with an artist to create a collage.

Groundwork Wirral and First Take Video Company worked with the local community to produce a reminiscence video celebrating the rich history of the Ilchester Square area. Local people shared memories and stories from the Dock Cottages era, the Ilchester Square flats and Lee's Tapestry Works.

A forum for older members of the community is currently being established and Groundwork Wirral will be continuing work with local schools about the heritage of the area and Lee's Tapestry factory.

Through the video community pride in the neighbourhood and its past will be communicated to younger generations.

Groundwork Wirral is part of a national Federation of 48 Groundwork trusts in England, Wales and Northern Ireland who seek to build sustainable communities through joint environmental action.
Groundwork Wirral can be contacted on 0151-644-4700

WIRRAL